The United Nations

Sean Connolly

W
FRANKLIN WATTS

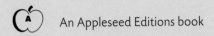
An Appleseed Editions book

First published in 2008 by Franklin Watts
338 Euston Road, London NW1 3BH

Franklin Watts Australia
Hachette Children's Books
Level 17/207 Kent St, Sydney, NSW 2000

Created by Appleseed Editions Ltd,
Well House, Friars Hill, Guestling,
East Sussex TN35 4ET

Designed by Helen James
Edited by Mary-Jane Wilkins
Picture research by Su Alexander

ISBN 978 07496 8068 8

Dewey Classification: 341.23

A CIP catalogue for this book is available from the British Library.

Photograph acknowledgements
page 6 UN photo; 9, 11 & 12 Bettmann/Corbis; 13 Hulton Deutsch
Collection/Corbis; 15 UN photo; 16 Paulo Figueiras/UN; 18 Reuters/Corbis;
21 Eskinder Debebe/UN; 22 Arne Hodalic/Corbis; 24 Mark Garten/UN;
25 & 26 Jean Pierre Laffont/UN; 27 John Isaac/UN; 28 Hector Mata/AFP/
Getty Images; 31 Lisbon City Museum/Handout/Reuters/Corbis; 33 Arko
Datta/Reuters/Corbis; 34 Paula Bronstein/Getty Images; 37 Sion Touhig/Corbis;
38 Bettmann/Corbis; 39 INA/Pool_AP_INA/EPA/Corbis; 41 Getty Images
Front cover David Turnley/Corbis

Printed in Hong Kong

Franklin Watts is a division of Hachette Children's Books

CONTENTS

A world free of war and problems?

Imagine a world with no more war. People could resolve their differences by talking them over freely and calmly. Imagine a world in which everyone was offered a good education, decent food and the best health care.

Most young people find it easy to imagine such a world. They feel that the present world's wars, hunger, illness and ignorance can be changed. Too often, though, the aims and idealism of childhood fade as people become older. Many adults believe it is impossible to change

This sculpture, Non-violence, stands outside United Nations HQ in New York City. The sculptor, Karl Fredrik Reutersward, used a twisted gun to symbolize the UN's efforts to build peace.

the world in the way their children dream about. They come to accept problems as simply part of life, and decide that nothing can be done about them.

A real force for good

Luckily, not everyone accepts the way things are. Individuals and organizations look at the same problems and try to find realistic ways of solving them. The most important of these organizations is the United Nations (UN), a group of 192 of the world's countries. The UN devotes itself to peace, friendship and improving the way of life of the world's neediest people.

The United Nations has proved to be a real and practical force for good since it began more than 60 years ago. The countries that joined forces to found the UN were nearing the end of a terrible war. The main purpose of their new organization was to promote and preserve peace. They knew that this would be a difficult goal to achieve, but the alternative – another war like the one they had witnessed – was too dreadful to consider. These countries gave the United Nations tools and money to help it achieve its original aim, as well as the aims drawn up later, which reflect the UN's growing role in the world.

No pleasing everyone

The United Nations has had a number of successes, but it has also been criticized and has even made some enemies. The UN has played a part in many of the world's conflicts in the last six decades – not always successfully. Could it have done things differently? Would another organization have been more successful? Would the world be better off without the UN, so that countries had to look after themselves and to resolve their own differences? This book raises some of these questions and also looks at the inner workings of this huge organization.

Setting the scene

The beginning of the twentieth century was a time of great change. The Industrial Revolution had transformed the way many people lived – not always for the better. Factories produced more goods than ever, but many people worked in grim conditions for poor wages.

People could buy products they had never seen before – such as cars, radios and electric lights – but other new products included weapons that were far deadlier than anything used in the past.

At the same time, Europe's most powerful countries seemed to be slipping towards war because of an ever-tightening web of treaties and alliances. When the First World War began in 1914, there was a new and more damaging type of fighting. Aeroplanes and tanks took the fighting into places far from traditional battlefields. Powerful bombs, machine guns and poison gas showed how industrial advances could be used against people.

By the time the First World War ended in 1918, about ten million people (many of them civilians) had died. Most leaders in Europe, (where much of the fighting had taken place) tried to find ways to avoid another such war. But what could they do to achieve their aim?

The League of Nations

Many people described the First World War as 'the war to end all wars' even while it was happening. When it ended, European leaders hoped to prevent such a war ever happening again. The countries which had been involved – both winners and losers – took part in a peace conference that set out ways of avoiding another world war.

Millions of soldiers had to spend months – or even years – camped in trenches along the front line during the First World War. Many lost their lives in battles that moved the line just a few metres in either direction.

Where was America?

The League of Nations faced problems from the start because it lacked a particular member – the United States. By the time of the First World War (in which the USA took part for about a year), the United States had become the most powerful country in the world. Without the United States the League of Nations lacked real power and influence in the wider world.

The absence of the USA was strange because US President Woodrow Wilson was one of the leaders who first came up with the idea of the league. In 1918 he made a speech in which he outlined 14 points which would lead to European peace – forming a League of Nations was the last and most important of these points.

Others in America disagreed with Wilson. They believed that the United States had made a mistake in entering the First World War, in which 116,000 Americans died. They believed that the war had been a European affair and no business of America's. President Wilson met opposition in the US Congress but still hoped to convince the American people. In 1919 he set off on a lengthy tour of his country, travelling 13,000 km in 22 days and giving 38 speeches.

The tour proved too much for President Wilson, who suffered a serious stroke in October 1919. He struggled on as president for another year, but did not have enough support to enable the United States to enter the league.

One of these ways was to set up an organization that would help countries settle their differences without going to war. The League of Nations was established on 28 June 1919. Representatives of 44 countries signed the Charter that gave birth to the league, and from 1920 it was based in Geneva.

Like the United Nations, the League of Nations had three main parts:
• a secretariat (to offer leadership and to oversee how the league was run);
• a council (to decide on matters relating to war and peace);
• an assembly (so every member country had a voice during annual meetings).

The league also established a number of smaller organizations which focused on other international problems, such as health, labour, justice and slavery.

Many people think that the League of Nations failed (see pages 12-14), but it did pave the way for the United Nations. Although it didn't prevent the Second World War,

it did succeed in some other areas. The International Labour Organization helped to introduce an eight-hour working day in many countries and fought to improve working conditions for women and young people. The Health Organization helped to slow or prevent the spread of deadly diseases, especially an outbreak of typhus in eastern Europe. It also helped nearly half a million refugees, whose lives had been turned upside down by the First World War.

US President Woodrow Wilson spent much of 1919 touring the US to build support for the League of Nations. The trip was a failure: Wilson did not get the backing of Congress and his own health failed.

WHAT DO YOU THINK?

The missing link?
Can you think of any other reasons why many Americans wanted no part of the League of Nations after the First World War? Were these reasons good enough to justify staying out of the league?

The birth of the UN

An international organization is only as powerful as its members – and the respect they have for it. The League of Nations failed in both these areas.

Ethiopian leader Haile Selassie appealed directly to the League of Nations for help after Italian forces invaded his country in 1936.

Without the most powerful country (the United States) on board, the league lacked real authority. Other powerful countries were only members briefly: Germany from 1926 to 1933 and the Soviet Union from 1934 to 1940.

Just as worrying was the fact that some member countries chose to ignore the League of Nations. In January 1923, France took over the Ruhr Valley, a major German industrial region. Soon afterwards, Italy attacked the Greek island of Corfu. The League of Nations took no action against either, which threatened to withdraw from the league if action was taken against them. When the league criticized Japan for invading Manchuria in 1933, Japan withdrew from the league. Two years later, the league failed to stop Italy's invasion of Ethiopia.

Another global war

All this military action signalled that another world war was likely – and the League of Nations was unable to stop it. The Second World War began in 1939, and the league did not meet during the war years. This war was even bloodier than the first: more than 60 million people (including 37 million civilians) died: 2.5 per cent of the world's people.

In August 1945, weeks before the war ended, the United States dropped two atomic bombs on Japan. The US argued that these bombs forced the Japanese to surrender earlier and saved thousands of lives. But the world had caught a glimpse of how devastating another war might be. It became even more important to build an international effort for peace.

Much of Europe lay in ruins as a result of the destruction of the Second World War. Only a shell remained of Coventry Cathedral (below), which had stood for more than 500 years.

Noble aims

The opening phrases of the United Nations Charter make its aims very clear:
'We the peoples of the United Nations determined to save succeeding generations from the scourge of war, which twice in our lifetime has brought untold sorrow to mankind, and to reaffirm faith in fundamental human rights, in the dignity and worth of the human person, in the equal rights of men and women and of nations large and small, and to establish conditions under which justice and respect for the obligations arising from treaties and other sources of international law can be maintained, and to promote social freedom and better standards of life in larger freedom...'

The UN is born

In late 1944, representatives of the five main Allies (France, China, the United Kingdom, the United States and the Soviet Union) had met for three months in the United States. They could sense victory in the war, but they had an even greater goal in mind – a way of turning that victory into a lasting peace. Their aim was to establish an organization that would succeed where the League of Nations failed. And that new organization was already being called the United Nations.

In April 1945, representatives of 50 countries met to turn the idea of a United Nations into reality. They tried to keep the best features of the League of Nations, while removing the parts that had failed so badly. The make-up of the United Nations (see pages 16–19) would give enormous influence and responsibilities to a few powerful countries – this move kept the United States interested. Like the league, the UN would have no permanent army, but it could call on its members to supply peacekeeping troops.

The Charter of the United Nations was signed on 26 June 1945. The UN (then known as the United Nations Organization) officially came into being on 24 October 1945, when a majority of the representative countries ratified it.

A new era of hope was born on 26 June 1945, when delegates signed the United Nations Charter in San Francisco. The Second World War had not ended, but the world looked to the new organization to build peace.

... ON THE SCENE ... ON THE SCENE ... ON THE SCENE ...

A four-day miracle

One of the UN's first successes was having its charter printed on time! The 282 representatives of the 50 countries attending the San Francisco conference kept changing the wording of the charter until 22 June 1945. That left the printers with just four days to produce a 145-page document in five languages. Usually they would take three months to complete such a job.

Fifty years after the event, Joe Baxley returned to the University of California printing office, where he had helped to print the charter. He had a clear memory of the chaos and rush of that four-day period, when people got by on just a few hours' sleep. 'They kept us busy setting the text, sending out proofs and getting an endless series of revised proofs in each of the five languages – English, French, Spanish, Russian and Chinese. Different people would ask for proofs and we'd get different corrections. At one point, nobody knew what… was going on.'

When the charter was finally printed, reporters and photographers from around the world came to interview the team who had worked this miracle. 'Unfortunately, the printers and staff who had actually been involved… were at home asleep, recuperating from their exhausting experience,' said Baxley.

A global reach

Since the first countries signed up to form the United Nations in 1945, the organization has grown to include 192 member nations today.

The only non-members are Taiwan, Kosovo, Northern Cyprus, Western Sahara, Palestine and Vatican City, and each of these has an unofficial presence at the UN. But although the UN has grown dramatically, its structure today is very similar to the 1945 version.

What the United Nations aims to do...

The aims of the United Nations are set out in its charter, to which every country must agree before becoming a member. The charter

The UN General Assembly in session: each of the 192 member nations sends a representative, or ambassador, to take part in debates and to vote on major issues.

Organs of the United Nations

The main UN elements are often called organs, like the lungs and heart of a human body. They are as follows.

The General Assembly

Each of the 192 members sends a representative to the General Assembly, which is like a parliament. Each country has a single vote on General Assembly issues. Although its decisions are not binding, the General Assembly is a good reflection of world opinion: governments sometimes choose to change their behaviour once they realize how it offends other countries.

The Security Council

This is the organ devoted to preserving peace. It has 15 members, five of which are permanent members (China, France, Russia, the UK and the USA). The ten other members are elected by the General Assembly for two-year terms. All five permanent members (sometimes called the Big Five) must agree on important decisions.

The Secretariat

This organ is the heart (or brain) of the United Nations, responsible for making sure the UN runs smoothly. At its head is the Secretary-General, who helps to guide the work of all UN organs and who travels the world to promote peace and well-being.

Economic and Social Council

This council, often called ECOSOC, advises the other UN organs about ways to promote higher standards of living and human rights. Its 54 members are elected by the General Assembly and serve three-year terms.

The Trusteeship Council

This branch of the UN helped the former colonies of countries that had been defeated in the Second World War. By 1994 its job was completed when the tiny Pacific country of Palau became independent. It still exists although it has no role.

International Court of Justice

Unlike the other five organs, which are based in the UN headquarters in New York City, the International Court of Justice is based in The Hague, Netherlands. The court consists of 15 judges who are elected by the General Assembly and who serve nine-year terms. It settles legal disputes submitted by countries or by international organizations.

states that the UN aims to promote peace and security, economic and social development, and human rights. These aims form the core of the United Nations. Together, they take countries that might be divided along religious, political or cultural lines and help them draw together – or, to put it another way, to become more united.

...and what the United Nations cannot do

The United Nations does not interfere in events taking place inside a country because it recognizes the sovereignty of its members. It cannot enforce its policies inside a country even if that country is ruled by a dictator. This set of limits shows that the United Nations is not – and never aimed to be – a world government. Instead it concentrates on improving relations between countries and throughout the world.

Slobodan Milosovic, the former leader of Serbia and Yugoslavia, was arrested in 2000. He was accused of crimes against humanity because of his role in wars in the region. His case was still being decided by the UN International Court of Justice when he died in 2006.

... ON THE SCENE ... ON THE SCENE ... ON THE SCENE ...

The newest member

On 28 June 2006, representatives of the 191 United Nations member states listened as General Assembly President Jan Eliasson called for approval of a new resolution – that the United Nations accept a new member. He asked anyone with an objection to speak up. When no one objected, Eliasson banged his gavel and said 'I declare the Republic of Montenegro admitted to membership in the United Nations.' The other diplomats burst into loud applause as Montenegro became the 192nd member of the United Nations.

The process had been surprisingly quick. On 21 May 2006, voters in Montenegro (part of former Yugoslavia) chose to separate from Serbia. Montenegro declared its independence officially on 3 June. Two days later, Montenegro's President, Filip Vujanovic, applied for UN membership by sending a letter to UN Secretary-General Kofi Annan.

The UN rules state that a country can be admitted by the General Assembly, which in turn acts on the recommendation of the Security Council.

On 16 June, the Secretary-General passed on the Montenegro application to the Security Council, which set up a committee to study the application before recommending approval to the General Assembly. The 'no objections' question on 28 June was the last step before Montenegro could join the largest community of nations.

WHAT DO YOU THINK?

A new role

One international organization has called for the Trusteeship Council to be put in charge of 'global commons' (the oceans, Antarctica and the atmosphere) that do not belong to any country. Do you think this would be a good idea?

Keeping the peace

Born during the last days of the most brutal war in history, the United Nations has been devoted to promoting peace from the first day.

There may be only a few people alive who fought in the Second World War (and only a handful of survivors of the First World War), but the images and legacies of those conflicts remain. And because even deadlier weapons have been developed since 1945, many experts believe that the human race would not survive a third world war.

Taking real action

The United Nations describes peacekeeping as 'a way to help countries torn by conflict to create conditions for sustainable peace'. Like the League of Nations before it, the UN has no armed forces of its own to patrol the world's trouble spots. But unlike the league, the UN can call on its members to send their own troops into these areas. These troops remain in their national uniforms, but wear the distinctive blue helmet of UN peacekeepers.

... ON THE SCENE ... ON THE SCENE ... ON THE SCENE ...

Lasting memories

Marianne Doyle was a 22-year-old serving with the Australian Navy when she was sent to the island of East Timor in 1999. East Timor had been a Portuguese colony, but was invaded by Indonesia in 1975. After more than two decades of struggle, the East Timorese had won the chance to decide for themselves whether to remain part of Indonesia.

When most East Timorese voted for independence in August 1999, pro-Indonesia militias responded with fierce attacks. The United Nations sent a peacekeeping mission, led by Australia, on 25 October 1999, to help the young country adjust to independence.

Marianne Doyle was part of that operation, sometimes using her nursing training. The experience has stayed with her ever since: 'Our job was to rebuild anything we could. It was a matter of pulling buildings apart to make a whole building. We were working with scrap, pretty much. We rebuilt a wing of a hospital and re-roofed a school.

'One day a little boy followed us for miles and wouldn't say what he wanted. Finally we sat down to have a drink and that was it, he wanted fresh water. We gave him a bottle and he was so excited, he ran off with it.

'It does make you look at your own life and think how incredibly lucky you are.'

Children in East Timor play among UN peacekeepers. The United Nations has helped to build peace in this young country, which had suffered terribly during its 30-year fight for independence.

The Security Council decides when and where UN peacekeeping missions should be set up. It also determines the size of a force needed to make an effective contribution. Member countries volunteer their own troops to form a peacekeeping team. Since the first operation (in the Middle East) in 1948, the United Nations has organized 60 peacekeeping missions. In late 2006, almost 90,000 people were serving in 18 different UN peacekeeping operations.

Bullet-holes dot a sign outside a Bosnian school. The United Nations tried to control the bitter fighting that tore Bosnia apart in the early 1990s.

WHAT DO YOU THINK?

Could the killing have been prevented?

The United Nations was closely involved in trying to end a vicious civil war which raged in the eastern European country of Bosnia between 1992 and 1995. The war developed after the larger country of Yugoslavia (which had included Bosnia and five of its neighbours) broke apart in 1991.

The path to independence in Bosnia was bloody, with two main groups (Bosnian Muslims and Bosnian Serbs) struggling for control. UN peacekeepers arrived in June 1992. The fighting continued and by 1993, Serbian armed forces were threatening several Muslim population centres, including the region around the town of Srebrenica. The United Nations responded by declaring Srebrenica a safe haven, where there should be no fighting.

Serbian forces continued to move in on Srebrenica. In 1995, the UN commander in Bosnia, General Bertrand Janvier of France, asked the UN to send in many more soldiers or to remove the UN force in Srebrenica so that the Serbian positions could be attacked from the air. The United Nations failed to do either of these things and the Serbian forces captured Srebrenica.

What followed was one of the worst massacres in Europe since the Second World War. Thousands of Bosnian Muslims were rounded up and as many as 8,000 were brutally executed. Can you think of any way that the United Nations could have prevented this slaughter?

The United Nations is called on to keep the peace, and not to make it. The UN Security Council depends on the cooperation of the countries involved for its peacekeeping missions. Usually, the parties involved have signed a treaty; UN peacekeepers can then enter the former war zone to make sure that the treaty takes effect.

Just what the peacekeepers must do depends on the mission. In some cases, the 'blue helmets' form a visible presence in a trouble spot as other soldiers are withdrawn from the area. Other peacekeepers might be observers as a country or region – until recently caught up in fighting – has elections. Some peacekeepers are police officers, helping local police forces to develop in areas that have been lawless for years.

The United Nations sent peacekeepers to the border between Israel and Lebanon after it set up a ceasefire in August 2006. Southern Lebanon had become a battlefield in the weeks before the ceasefire.

Human rights

An Indonesian girl wakes before dawn, eats a bowl of rice and then works a 12-hour shift in a shoe factory. Government forces in Bolivia move in on a farmers' demonstration and open fire. Families are forced from their homes in Angola to live in tent villages.

Children must leave school and begin working when they are still very young in many parts of the world. These girls from Mauritania, in West Africa, spend their days working together to make straw rugs.

What connects these events and others like them, which take place every day around the world? The answer is that each is a violation of a basic human right. Some of the most fundamental human rights include education, access to health care and justice, and the chance to find a job. People in many countries take these rights for granted

These boys spend hours carrying bricks by hand at a building site in New Delhi, in India. The United Nations works to improve living conditions for young people like them.

because they have not been threatened in anyone's memory. But in other parts of the world, human rights are only a cherished dream for people whose lives are a miserable, cruel routine.

Taking stock

The huge loss of life in the Second World War was one of the reasons the United Nations was formed. But it was also clear that human rights – or the lack of them – lay at the heart of that global war. Millions of people died because some governments (especially that of Nazi Germany) refused to accept the basic qualities and needs that all people share.

Protecting these rights, or developing them in countries where they have been ignored, is a major aim of the United Nations. In 1948, the UN General Assembly adopted the Universal Declaration of Human Rights. This declaration was a response to the cruelty of the Second World War. Although it is only a guideline – and not enforced as law – it spells out the basic rights and freedoms every human being should enjoy. The UN described these as part of the 'foundation of freedom, justice and peace in the world.'

Girls in Pakistan share text books as they practise reading and spelling. Increasing literacy (the ability to read and write) around the world is one of the most important UN goals for young people.

Making progress

The United Nations has a separate department (the Office of the High Commissioner for Human Rights, or OHCHR) that devotes itself to human rights around the world. The OHCHR studies human rights in every country. It aims to improve conditions for those who are worst off while protecting those who do enjoy some rights.

... ON THE SCENE ... ON THE SCENE ... ON THE SCENE ...

Taken to be a slave

Sia Mondeh was only ten years old when rebel forces in her native Sierra Leone kidnapped her. The West African country was in the middle of a bitter civil war, and young people were taken from their families to work almost as slaves in other parts of the country. Luckily for Sia, her case was reported to members of a UN peacekeeping mission in Sierra Leone.

The UN peacekeepers had a special responsibility to promote human rights throughout Sierra Leone, to strengthen a treaty made in 1999 which stopped the fighting. But young people like Sia were stranded and living in dreadful conditions. The UN workers, helped by local police, conducted an investigation. Eventually they discovered the whereabouts of Sia's family and she was reunited with them after five years of separation.

Opposite page
Protesters call for the United Nations to help the people of Tibet. Once independent, Tibet has been under strict Chinese control since 1959. Many observers accuse China of crushing human rights in Tibet.

There is only so much the OHCHR can do, as the United Nations cannot force countries to change. However, it has set up a number of special procedures to study human rights and report back. Some of these special procedures involve sending a team to a country (such as Cuba, Somalia or Cambodia) to report on the human rights position as a whole in that nation. Other special procedures focus on international themes such as the right to food, education and freedom of religion. Half way through 2006, there were 41 special procedures in place.

The OHCHR uses information from the special procedures to put pressure on other UN branches (for example, peacekeepers) and on other international agencies involved in the areas where human rights are under threat. This pressure can help the other organization or UN branch to press for human rights.

WHAT DO YOU THINK?

Right about rights?

The Caribbean island nation of Cuba has been at odds with the United States since Fidel Castro set up a communist government there in 1959. Castro's government has stifled many aspects of democracy, such as free elections, and the US blocked all trade with Cuba in 1962. Cuba's economy would improve if it could trade with the US, but the US will not trade unless Cuba improves its record on human rights.

Supporters of Cuba say that human rights — and other signs of democracy — would improve if the United States began trading first. They also say that the US position is unfair, especially since the United States supports many countries with far worse human rights records than Cuba. The American position, they say, is interfering with Cuba's right to govern itself. What do you think?

Help on many fronts

The United Nations, according to the opening words of its charter, aims to build 'better standards of life' around the world. Just as parents want the best for their children, the founders of the United Nations want their 'offspring' (future generations) to have more to eat, a better chance of finding work and a better chance of staying healthy.

The process of improving living conditions is called development, and the United Nations devotes much energy to this aim. Its international status makes it easier for the UN to focus on those countries and regions that need special help. Some of them might have lagged behind other parts of the world because they had been colonies for many decades. Others have suffered under cruel or selfish rulers who paid little attention to the needs of the people of the country.

Knowing who needs help is one thing; giving them help and advice is another. The United Nations Development Programme (UNDP) is in charge of the UN's efforts in this area. The UNDP provides advice, training and funds to help countries reduce poverty; promote democracy and equality (especially for women); combat HIV/AIDS; protect the environment; save energy; and prepare for natural disasters.

The UNDP sometimes gives money to countries for development, but its most important role is to identify problems and outline solutions. Then it can tap its international experience and expertise to work alongside governments or other international organizations. These partnerships can help people in developing countries to become self-sufficient.

More than 60,000 people died in the Lisbon earthquake of 1755. Nowadays the United Nations helps to organize disaster relief in such emergencies, saving lives and caring for the injured.

... ON THE SCENE ... ON THE SCENE ... ON THE SCENE ...

A wave of terror

On 26 December 2004 a powerful earthquake just west of Indonesia sent several destructive tsunamis racing across the Indian Ocean. These towering waves came rushing into coastal areas, washing away whole towns and villages with no warning. More than 200,000 people died in the disaster and millions of people lost their homes.

The United Nations Children Fund (UNICEF) is one of the international organizations involved in helping those whose lives were changed in the disaster. Its Sri Lanka branch began concentrating on the psychological effects of the tsunami on the 30,000 children who were living in relief camps. Even months after the tsunami hit, many of these children were afraid to go near the sea because the memories were too painful. 'On that day I was playing next door at a neighbour's house,' recalls 14-year-old Jayakumar. 'I suddenly heard my mother screaming "the sea is coming. Get out. Run away."'

Jayakumar escaped, but both his mother and his younger brother died in the tsunami. Thanks to help and care from UNICEF, Jayakumar and his friends are beginning to smile and play again. This is the start of a return to normal life which helps the healing process: 'When we play we forget about everything. It is good for us to forget the bad things.'

Emergency action

The founders of the UN knew that parts of the world often face emergencies or long-term problems – these might be earthquakes or hurricanes, famine or drought. Up to the middle of the twentieth century, a country facing such a crisis would have dealt with it alone.

The number of casualties can increase rapidly after such a disaster – especially if the victims cannot reach medical treatment and emergency supplies. About 300,000 people died in floods following a typhoon that hit Calcutta, India, in 1737. More than 200,000 people died in the Kansu region of China after an earthquake in 1920.

The United Nations has a role to play in helping people recover and return to a normal life. Many different UN agencies can carry out emergency relief on the ground, but the UN has a special Emergency Relief Co-ordinator (ERC) to make sure that things happen quickly.

The UN uses the latest transport and communications systems to send help quickly. Cargo planes and helicopters, trucks and four-wheel drive vehicles take supplies and aid workers to an affected area. Once in place, these teams often build communications systems from scratch – power and telephone lines are often toppled in disasters. UN workers can mobilize wireless internet connections and mobile phone links to stay in touch and to organize relief efforts.

Survivors of the tsunami in December 2004 wash their clothes in a UN relief camp in Thirukkovil, along the east coast of Sri Lanka. Around 1.5 million Sri Lankans lost their homes in the tsunami, which killed more than 30,000 people on the island.

The Human Development Report

Every year since 1990, the United Nations Development Programme has produced a report that looks closely at every country and compares levels of development. This publication, the Human Development Report (HDR), has all the usual figures that experts expect: national income, levels of education and employment. But the HDRs go much further in painting a picture of each country. They measure how much freedom women have, how generous the country is to those who are less well-off, how many of a country's people can find fresh water easily. In short, the HDRs emphasize how people are affected.

One of the people who initiated the report was the Pakistani economist Mahbub ul Haq, who believed that people, rather than numbers, should be the cornerstone of development: 'The object of development is to create an enabling environment for people to enjoy long, healthy and creative lives.'

Opposite page
UNDP projects support
peaceful development around
the world. These former soldiers
are putting the finishing
touches to the roof of Chilstoon
Primary School in war-
torn Afghanistan. A UNDP
programme helped to pay
for the new school.

International links

In both development and emergency relief the UN has a history of co-operating with other international organizations, such as the World Bank, the World Health Organization (WHO) and the International Red Cross. Linking up ensures that none of these organizations (which share similar goals) duplicates the efforts of others.

An an example, International Red Cross teams arriving at the scene of an earthquake might share blankets and medical supplies with a UN team already on the ground. In return, the Red Cross team could use a communications system put in place by the UN group.

... ON THE SCENE ... ON THE SCENE ... ON THE SCENE ...

Ronaldo, Zidane and the UN

The 2010 Football World Cup Finals will be staged in South Africa. This is the first time an African country has had that honour. More than 300,000 visitors are expected at the event, and South Africa is already making preparations.

One of the most important plans is for a cleaner and healthier public transport system, which South Africans will be able to use long after the World Cup trophy is won. The UNDP has helped the South Africans to present a transport plan to the Global Environment Facility (GEF). If it goes ahead, the GEF could supply millions of dollars to help South Africa with the project.

On 28 August 2006, the plan went to the GEF Assembly, held in Cape Town, South Africa. It had support from two of the most famous footballers in the world, Brazil's Ronaldo and retired French star Zinedine Zidane. They signed a statement pointing out that the World Cup is about more than football. With billions of people watching around the world, it can be a showcase for new developments in the host country. More than that, a GEF-approved plan could suggest solutions for a cleaner, fairer, and ultimately more just planet.

Looking to the future

The United Nations has faced many challenges – and a rapidly changing world – since it was formed in 1945. After more than six decades, a third world war seems much less likely.

The cold war, which developed soon after the end of the Second World War, is now just another chapter in history. Few people now believe that the United States and Russia could lead the world to another (possibly deadly) conflict.

But as some challenges fade or are overcome, others appear or grow worse. Terrorism has become a huge concern for the United Nations and the world as a whole. Hunger, damage to the environment, HIV/AIDS and other killer diseases – all these are problems that pose an increasing threat to the world. And the UN faces some special challenges, from those who believe it is inefficient and even evil.

The Millennium Declaration

In September 2000, more than 150 heads of state met at UN headquarters in New York to discuss the future. Their gathering was called the UN Millennium Summit. At the end of four days of intense discussion – including some arguments – they all signed a detailed programme of action for the United Nations. This document, called the UN Millennium Declaration, has eight main targets which the UN aims to achieve by the year 2015.

Police scientists examine the wreckage of a London bus blown up in the terrorist attack of 7 July 2005. Three bomb explosions killed 56 people and injured more than 700.

The eight Millennium Declaration targets were:

• To rid the world of extreme poverty and hunger; to reduce hunger by half by 2015 and altogether by 2025

• To achieve universal primary education

• To promote equality between men and women and to ensure that girls and women have a chance to improve their own lives

• To ensure that fewer children die of diseases

• To improve the health of mothers

• To combat HIV/AIDS, malaria and other diseases

• To ensure that the environment is protected

• To develop a worldwide partnership for development

Each of these goals (called MDGs) costs money, and some are very expensive. Some experts estimate that it will cost about £21-32 billion every year to meet the goals.

The role of the United States

The most powerful country in the world has always had an up-and-down relationship with the UN. The land on which the UN headquarters was built, in one of the most expensive districts of New York City, was a gift from American millionaire John D. Rockefeller, Jr in 1946. The USA was a keen supporter of the UN in its early days.

Opposite page
John D. Rockefeller, Jr gave the UN more than $8 million dollars which paid for the building of their headquarters along the East River in New York City in 1949. Americans supported the UN wholeheartedly at that time.

Many people believe that Saddam Hussein, the former leader of Iraq, used UN money to become rich and to remain in power from 1995 to 2003.

In return, it enjoyed the support of most other UN members in its foreign action – especially during the Korean War of the early 1950s.

There have always been Americans who distrust large international groups. They share the views of those who voted against the League of Nations and resent other countries 'telling us what to do'. They also believe that the United Nations is anti-Semitic because of its frequent criticism of Israel (an important US ally). Some Americans accuse the UN of wasting money because it is inefficient and corrupt (see What do you think?).

Part of the problem?

There are fierce critics and opponents of the UN in other countries too. Some agree with the view that the UN is not run properly and is open to all sorts of dishonesty. Others, who oppose any limits on their own country's power, see the United Nations as a world government which aims to force its views on everyone, whether they like it or not.

Opponents of the UN are hardly likely to welcome the £31 billion annual price tag that comes with the MDGs. They argue that the only real change occurs at local or regional levels. The best way to help starving people in East Africa, in their view, is to call on neighbouring African countries for help. For these people, it follows that involving the United Nations simply makes the problem worse.

Reform or wrecking?

In 2005 a dispute developed within the United Nations. Some large countries, such as the United States, threatened to withhold their contribution to the UN budget unless there were major changes. They argued that the Secretary-General should have more say in how the UN operates and how its money is spent. More than 130 smaller countries disagreed, arguing that the present system (in which the General Assembly has a great deal of control) is their only chance to have a say in how the UN operates. Who do you think was right?

Playing your part

Almost every person in the world lives in a country that is a member of the United Nations. And every person's country has a seat in the UN General Assembly and other UN committees and groups. Together, these representatives help to change the world.

But what about the people who live in the countries which do not sit in the United Nations General Assembly to debate world affairs? There are more than 6.5 billion of them and they also have a part to play. Adults in most countries can vote for governments which share their views about how to solve international problems. And a new government, once elected, appoints a UN ambassador to press for these solutions.

Millions of children in North America, Ireland and Hong Kong collect money for the UN Children's Agency (UNICEF) every year on Halloween. The 'Trick-or-treat for UNICEF' idea goes back to 1950. Since then, children have raised nearly £95 million.

A country's people can continue to press for change even in the years between elections. People can demonstrate, write to or e-mail their leaders, or use other legal activities to make people more aware of problems that the United Nations can address.

A role for the young

Young people can also play a part in helping the United Nations achieve its aims. They can take part in rallies and demonstrations about important issues, such as protecting the environment, fighting hunger and helping those with serious diseases.

One of the most important events is International Peace Day, which has been celebrated around the world on 21 September every year since 1982. Children – who benefit more than anyone from world peace – can participate in many peace-related activities on every Peace Day. Other events involve schools, families and adults.

Celebrating the UN

United Nations Day is celebrated in many countries on 24 October every year. This is the the date on which the United Nations officially came into being in 1945. The annual celebration gives people the chance to learn more about the goals, history and achievements of the UN.

Some countries take a particular interest in marking United Nations Day. In Costa Rica it is a national holiday. Other countries have different ways of honouring the United Nations on that day. Sweden, Denmark, Norway and Finland highlight 24 October as a flag day. It has also become a tradition for US presidents to issue a proclamation on that day, reminding Americans of how important the United Nations is and how the world benefits from its continuing success.

People also celebrate the United Nations and what it represents at a local level. The International School Singapore (ISS) has students from 40 countries who come from a wide range of cultures and backgrounds. One of the biggest events at the school every year is United Nations Night, which ties in with the 24 October observance. Students work together in national teams to plan and produce special performances for the Singapore community.

... ON THE SCENE ... ON THE SCENE ... ON THE SCENE ...

Pakistan for a day

Model United Nations events give young people the chance to experience what the UN is really like, and to take part.

Fifteen-year-old Jason Ham from Somerset had a chance to pursue two of his interests – politics and drama – when he took part in a Model United Nations (MUN) hosted by his school. Jason's MUN took place on 19 December 2005.

The four schools taking part had about four weeks to choose delegates, study countries and learn more about how the United Nations operates from day to day. Students learned how to prepare and propose resolutions, how to debate them and how votes are taken on these issues.

Jason represented Pakistan and joined the Health and Ecology Committee to debate issues such as HIV/AIDS, population growth and animal rights. He drew up resolutions on the War Against Terror and on zoos. But the session ran out of time because the debates on the other issues were so heated – so Jason's resolutions were never debated.

Despite having his resolutions shelved, Jason enjoyed the experience of putting himself in the position of another country and trying to think as someone from Pakistan might. Most importantly, 'the enthusiasm of all the delegates showed me that young people do care about the world, do care about life, and do care about respecting each and every person's point of view. I find that really exciting.'

WHAT DO YOU THINK?

Marking Peace Day
Does your school mark International Peace Day with a minute's silence every year on 21 September? If not, how could this activity be organized at school? Could any other peace-related activities (see links) work in your school or community?

Glossary

allies Individuals or countries who work together. During the Second World War, the Allies were countries led by France, China, the UK, the US and the Soviet Union, which opposed Germany, Japan and their partners.

ambassador Someone who represents his or her country in a foreign country.

anti-Semitic Opposed to, or supporting violence against, Jewish people.

atomic bomb A powerful bomb which releases nuclear energy.

charter A written document that describes how an organization operates.

cold war A period lasting roughly from 1945 to 1991 during which the United States and the Soviet Union opposed each other and nearly went to war several times.

colony A region of the world controlled or governed by an outside country.

communist Someone who believes in a system in which all property is owned by the community and each person contributes and receives according to their ability and needs. A communist government provides work, health care, education and housing, but may deny people certain freedoms.

Congress The branch of the US government (like the British Parliament) in which elected representatives decide on laws.

corrupt Dishonest (often in a way that involves taking money for some official action).

First World War A war fought mainly in Europe between 1914 and 1918.

gavel A wooden hammer banged down during a meeting to announce a decision.

head of state The most senior person who can represent a country elsewhere, eg the British queen, or the US president. A head of state need not be part of a government.

HIV/AIDS HIV stands for human immunodeficiency virus, which causes AIDS (acquired immune deficiency syndrome), a virus passed on in blood and sexual fluids.

idealism A belief that the best things possible can be achieved.

Industrial Revolution A period beginning in Britain in the 18th century, when new inventions changed how things were made. Machines often did the work of humans.

malaria A serious illness, often deadly, spread to human beings by mosquitoes.

Manchuria A region of China invaded and ruled by Japan from 1931 to 1945.

militia A small group of armed people.

Nazi The political party of Adolf Hitler, who led Germany into the Second World War. Nazis believed that Germans were superior to others (including Jews, gypsies and the handicapped) who should be moved out or killed.

proofs The draft of a printed work, produced so mistakes can be corrected.

ratified Agreed officially.

scourge Something that causes great trouble or suffering.

Second World War A war waged around the world in which the Allies fought against Germany, Japan and their partners.

secretariat The branch of an organization that includes the leader and his or her staff.

Soviet Union The name given to a country that included Russia and 14 of its neighbours, which united to form a larger communist country from 1917 to 1991.

stroke The blockage of a blood vessel in the brain, leading to serious physical and mental problems and even death.

sustainable Able to be continued without stopping.

terrorism Using violence to force governments to agree to demands.

violation A breaking of the rules.

World Bank A bank which lends money to help poorer countries develop.

Further reading

The Role of the United Nations (*In the News* series) S Adams (Franklin Watts, 2004)

Keeping Peace in the World (*What's Your View?* series) A Hibert (Franklin Watts, 2006)

Children Just Like Me A Kindersley (Dorling Kindersley, 2006)

United Nations (*World Watch* series) S Ross (Hodder, 2003)

For Every Child UNICEF (Arrow Books, 2000)

Websites

http://www.internationaldayofpeace.org/
A site devoted to the annual Day of Peace (21 September).

http://cyberschoolbus.un.org/modelun/index.asp
The Model United Nations pages reveal the fun – as well as the educational benefits – of taking part in MUN events.

http://www.un.org/Pubs/ourlives/main.htm
UN history, aims and achievements. Packed with information and first-hand accounts.

http://cyberschoolbus.un.org/cyberschoolbus/index.shtml
Information, interviews and interactive games, plus links to UN sites and beyond.

Index